THE GARDEN
GOING ON
WITHOUT US

Lorna Crozier

THE GARDEN
GOING ON
WITHOUT US

M&S

Canadian Cataloguing in Publication Data

Crozier, Lorna, 1948 –
  The garden going on without us

Poems.
ISBN 0-7710-2475-4

I. Title.

PS8555.R72G37   1985   C811.'54   C85-099154-4
PR9199.3.C769G37   1985

The publishers acknowledge the support given by the Canada
Council for the Arts and the Ontario Arts Council for their
publishing program.

Set in Perpetua by The Typeworks, Vancouver
Printed and bound in Canada

McClelland & Stewart Inc.
The Canadian Publishers
481 University Avenue
Toronto, Ontario
M5G 2E9

  3 4 5   02 01 00 99 98

For Patrick

Contents

III

THE MORNING OF THE SAD WOMEN

IV

THE GARDEN GOING ON WITHOUT US

V

WHAT THE MIND TURNS OVER

I

Forms of Innocence

TAUTOLOGIES OF SUMMER

Every morning there are sparrows
and rhubarb leaves. Somewhere
a heron mimics shadows

while desire moves
just below the surface.
In spite of pain

desire repeats itself
again and again
like the snake who

looking for its lost skin
traces its shape in the sand
simply by moving forward.

In this cold country
our angels are made of snow
and no one talks about them.

The man will not speak of his enchantment
with their long hair
that sweeps across the car lights.
The woman will not tell you
of their hands — how large and strong they look
as if they too raised children, planted seeds
and carried water from a well.

They live in our country
during the longest season.
Around the barns and sheds,
in stubble fields, under frozen rivers.

Sometimes when the yardlight
splits the darkness
you see them outside the window,
pressed against the frozen pane,
wanting in.

It is then you don't like to be alone.
You feel the coldness of their wings
even though they sing so beautifully
they have silenced the dog
who runs in circles
at the end of his chain,
blinded by their brilliance.

POEM ABOUT NOTHING

Zero is the one we didn't understand
at school. Multiplied by anything
it remains nothing.

When I ask my friend
the mathematician who studies rhetoric
if zero is a number, he says *yes*
and I feel great relief.

If it were a landscape
it would be a desert.
If it had anything to do
with anatomy, it would be
a mouth, a missing limb,
a lost organ.

ø

Zero worms its way
                        between one and one
and changes everything.
It slips inside the alphabet.
It is the vowel on a mute tongue,
the pupil in a blind man's eye,
the image
            of the face
he holds on his fingertips.

ø

When you look up
from the bottom of a dry well

zero is what you see,
the terrible blue of it.

It is the rope
you knot around your throat
when your heels itch for wings.

Icarus understood zero
as he caught the smell
of burning feathers
and fell into the sea.

ø

If you roll zero down a hill
it will grow,
swallow the towns, the farms,
the people at their tables
playing tic-tac-toe.

ø

When the Cree chiefs
signed the treaties on the plains
they wrote X
beside their names.

In English, X equals zero.

ø

I ask my friend
the rhetorician who studies mathematics
What does zero mean and keep it simple.

He says *Zip.*

ø

Zero is the pornographer's number.
He orders it through the mail
under a false name. It is the number
of the last man on death row,
the number of the girl who jumps
three stories to abort.

Zero starts and ends
at the same place. Some compare it
to driving across the Prairies all day
and feeling you've gone nowhere.

ø   ø   ø

In the beginning God made zero.

The horizon is a line
written by a madman,
a long run-on sentence,
the letters so small and crabbed
even he can't read them.

With a felt-tip pen
he begins at a spot
marked "Start here"
and with his whole body
pushes the line around the world.

Sometimes he gets lost,
distracted. You'll wake
to find a thin black stripe
across your house, your car,
your white cat.

That's when the world
gets out of kilter.
You step into a day
so clear, so full of light,
you know you're in a different place,
the horizon indecipherable
but closer
than it's ever been before.

FORMS OF INNOCENCE

The girl can tell you exactly
where and when her innocence
took flight,
how it soared from the window
beating its wings
high above the stubble field.

A strange shape for innocence
when you think of Leda
but this girl insists
it was a swan, black
not white as you might expect.
From its head no bigger than her fist
a beak blossomed red as if wings
pumped blood up the long neck
to where the bird split the sky.

She watched this through the windshield,
lying on her back, the boy's breath
breaking above her in waves, the swan's
dark flight across the snow so beautiful
she groaned and the boy groaned with her,
not understanding the sound she made.

When she tells this story now, she says
though it was winter, she knows the swan
made it all the way to Stanley Park,
a place she's never been, just seen
in the room where no one
ever touches anything

in the book her mother keeps
open on the coffee table,
one black swan swimming
endless circles among the white.

THE FOETUS DREAMS

1

Lungs.
It dreams heart.
Spleen. Liver.
It dreams two faces:

one it will wear
before it is born.

2

In the morning
the foetus dreams the sun.
It pushes against red walls
wanting to touch light
with pale buds of fingers.

There is no sun.

The foetus dreams
the shadow of a cloud
bruises its eyelids.
It hears rain
tapping on the forehead
of its mother.
It dreams
it is a fish that swims
in her laughter
through the seasons
of her blood.

3

The foetus dreams
wind fills its skin-bag,
lifts it out and up

an ocular *o*

round and clear
as a bubble blown
from a child's ring.

The earth shrinks
to a speck of dust
under a new-formed nail.
Stars like fireflies
catch in its fine
black hair.

4

The foetus dreams
it is a whisper
sealed in a clear jar
set on a kitchen shelf
where a red geranium
presses its petals
against glass skin
until night turns
the window cold and dark.

5

The foetus dreams a man
hangs a moonstone around its mother's throat.

It dreams a man
follows her through the shadows of the park,

stands outside her bedroom window,
leaves his breath in circles on the pane.

It dreams a man with a face it has known
moves his mouth in words across her belly.

It cries and kicks
                    the voice away
beating the stretched skin like a drum.

6

The foetus dreams a name
it fills like a round
glass or a mouth.
It moves like light
into the spaces defined
by the letters. It moves
like breath into the spaces
between the letters.

It grows within the name
as ice expands in stone
fissures

       yet the stone holds
and will not break.

7

The foetus dreams it is
a black hole
       cut into the tinny blue.
It dreams someone
cuts off its foot for a dime,
someone splits its tongue
so it can say a word. It dreams
it sits on its mother's hip
while she lies sleeping. In the dawn
it flies away
       with her black
and dreaming eyes.

8

It dreams it is a mouth,
a fish swimming in a mouth.
It dreams its mother
hooks a fish.
She reels it in
on a long thin vein
she winds
round and round her wrist.

24

9

The foetus dreams it is a man.
It dreams it is a woman.
It dreams it is half
                and half.
It dreams it is unhappy.
It dreams two pains: one
will not stop after the foetus
squeezes from the vise,
the tight tunnel.

It wants to be
a thing with wings
that says one word
                over and over.

10

The woman turns in sleep,
the foetus turns. She dreams
a thing inside her.
It eats her heart.
It chews through her belly.
It splits her in two
like an avocado, a stone
rolls out. It is a fish
with teeth, a bird with spurs,
a plant that roots in her lungs.
It rides out of her
on a black horse,
it cries *Mother*.

CHILDHOOD

Close your eyes for a moment,
listen:
the floorboards groan at your mother's step,
bread pans scrape the oven grate,
her fingers tap the crust.
Where are you now?
Pretending sleep in another room
where windows turn dreams to frost,
feather forests, the birds are white
and make no sound.

Listen: your mother pours milk in a cup.
It holds the light like a small lamp,
draws shadows from her face.
Where have you gone?
Your mother is calling.
Your name is warmed by her breath.
Snow fills your tracks,
turns everything into a softer shape,
a silence, forgiveness.

Come in for supper,
it is growing dark.
A cup waits for you, a loaf of bread.
Your mother is calling, listen:
with her voice she builds a doorway
for you to enter, even now,
from such a long way off.

THE PHOTOGRAPH I KEEP OF THEM

He on a big Indian motorcycle
and she in the side-car.

It is before my brother
and long before I demanded
my own space in her belly.

Behind them the prairie
tells its spare story of drought.

They tell no stories.
Not how they feel
about one another
or the strange landscape
that makes them small.

I can write down only this
for sure:
> they have left the farm,
> they are going somewhere.

They said
   mice wear paths in the linoleum
   hide in the couch springs and
   under your bed wait for a chance
   to whoosh
      up your housecoat
   nest in your crotch

I learned to walk
   oriental style
I pressed my knees together
   until my thighs webbed

It will take a blade
thin as love sharp as dreams
to open me

LOVE SONG

Hair has a mind
of its own. At night
it lifts from your pillow
and mates with the wind.

That is why it is so knotted
and tangled in the morning,
why it breaks the teeth
of your finest combs,
spills from ribbons and barrettes.

It has spent
the night with the wind.
Can't you feel its wantonness
as it falls across your shoulders?

BADLANDS

We stand at the lip
of the great cavity
in the earth
It is night
The white and beige layers
of the hills glow

We have seen them
in the afternoon sun
Now they are different
This is a stronger pull

We want to dive
into darkness
                reach the centre
all the hills coil towards
Instead we lock fingers
hold one another
to the edge

Coyotes roll their voices
across the canyon
We lift our heads and howl
respond to the pack
cry our humanness away
howl with coyote wisdom

The pack moves on

There is something
we should say to each other
but our bare voices drop
to the silent
                empty pit

LETTER

Our first daughter
with pinking shears cut out her mouth,
stuck it on the mirror, a lipstick drawing,
then spoke her death. Our second daughter
swallowed a word I had carved into a hook,
then fell across the table, spilling
her wine on the white lace cloth.
The youngest son sewed my love
into his pockets and leapt into the dead
trees reaching from the river.
I keep their baby teeth in jars, hand
prints in books. All our children kill
themselves, I write.

PATCHWORK

The bed grew.
The empty half lay as stark
as a body coffined
on the dining-room table.

She wrinkled it
with different men
who left before morning
but from each she stitched
a piece into her heavy quilt —
the point of a tie
the pocket of a flowered shirt
ribbing from a wool vest
a leather square from a tobacco pouch
and once the skin from the back of a hand
with the soft tattoo
of a bee's back.

STILL LIFE WITH NUDE

On this beach everyone
wants to be skinny
except the Rubens nude
sleeping in her flesh on the pier.

The sun is too small, her skin consumes it.
The movement of one foot is answered
by her whole body, ripples rising
up her thighs and belly, the waves of her hair.

When she gathers the light, billows past
the young women, thin in their bones,
she is a bright silk tent
breathing in and out
with wind off the water.

Inside its walls, a cat licks
the sweetness from an empty cup. Flies
dip their feet in the pulp of figs.
On red cushions a man kneels by a woman
who lifts her buttocks
round and glistening with sweat
in the perfumed light.

There is a story of a swan.
See the birthmark on the back of my neck
under my hair. That is where the great bird
pinched me in her beak, snatching me from the sea
and carrying my wet, salty body to the shore.
This is a story I could believe.
Sometimes the wings of a bird beat against
my skull. Feathers fill my mouth and eyes
with a whiteness like winter.

Or I was carried on a dolphin's back.
She pushed me to shore with her soft nose
then turned and disappeared under the waves,
the notes of her song hovering above the water.
In the blue light of evening, alone in the house,
I float through rooms, my sides sleek and slippery.

I was not made from a thin, dry rib
white and bare as if chewed and sucked
by a small dog. These breasts did not come
from a man's side, this round belly, this
hollow at the centre. We dreamed each other
at the same time and we dreamed a garden.
When we awoke there was wind in the leaves
above us apples glowing like red moons
as we turned to one another in the sweet green air.

Last night they came to visit.
One talked of women who dance
with balding men, wiggle
their asses to attract
those who sit
backs to the wall.
These new women
want to be blessed
with blood. They want men
who put their balls in glass
cases on display.

The other talked of rape,
men who turn
icons to the wall,
hold boiling water
above the woman's face
until she opens. *A fantasy,*
for a film about the Prairies.

This morning my lover and I
walk to the river to see the eclipse,
the last of this century, the last
before we die. We hold hands, watch
the joining of sun and moon.
A bat, thinking it is night,
stumbles into the sky.

II

Fishing in Air

LOVE POEM, AFTER RAIN

for Patrick

Eleven puff balls — no, twelve,
I must get it right —
swollen at the base of the pine
after last night's rain.

There were twelve
and I picked one,
brought it to you
lazy in bed.
                    Taste this,
and you bit it in two.

I rolled the other half
in my mouth, flicked
my tongue across
the shape of your teeth
in the mushroom's flesh.
Earth and darkness
and last night's rain.

THE APPLE TREE

1

The apple tree hums
white blossoms turn
yellow, honey bees carry
the shape of tree
up up in a buzzing
bloom high into the
high wind

2

How beautiful
the muted birds
as if a delicate finger
smudged the colours
into a haze, a grey whisper
the cedar waxwings dart
among branches
like leaf shadows moved
by wind they flutter
oh beautiful the birds
that feed on blossoms

3

Wind breathes through
the tree, loosens petals
into a butterfly's

brief flight
        they light
from birth to death
in a wing instant, a
sigh, the petals fall
— white silk rain

4

Someone says
        it's just like a wedding
        this white confetti
and we laugh
none of us believing
in weddings anymore
still we sit
where petals
settle in our hair
blessings
in the early
apple morning

My heart lies sleeping in the rushes
in a willow basket lined with cotton.

It is sleeping until it learns to be gentle.
It is sleeping until a woman lifts her skirts
and wades in the water to claim it
though it would rather live
in a red fox, a willow basket.

Lovers circle in the shape of swallows,
devour mosquitoes and the heart's malice.
Shooting stars trace its history across the sky.

In its dream it puts on feathers,
it puts on turquoise slippers.
In its dream it plays Billie Holiday
on a gramophone.

Put a finger to your lips, don't disturb
the angels dancing on the heart's pins.
In white rushes it is learning
to be gentle.

THIS IS A LOVE POEM WITHOUT RESTRAINT

This poem
is full of pain
full of pieces
It cries out
oh! oh! oh!
It has no pride
no discretion
It whimpers
It will not drop its eyes
when it meets a stranger
It will not hide
its tears

●

It will talk
of beauty
Lilacs Apples
The smell of rain
in caraganas
Your mouth
your eyes

What are you going to do about it?
You cannot stop me
now

●

The moon shines on this page
as the poem writes

itself. It is trying to find
whiteness
frost on snow
two feathers
on a pillow
your hands
          upon
my skin

                    •

These words are tired
of being
          words
They refuse to sit here
pretending
          they can't move
                         off the page

These are the first
ones to leave
their white space
They fall
on your tongue
letter
          by
                    letter
like raindrops

One of them
is my name

What will you do with it?
It has decided to live
inside you

                    •

This poem has no restraint
It will not say
plum blossom
sunset
rubbing stone
cat's cradle

It refuses to be evasive

I miss you
I miss you
Come home

•

It won't talk of passion
but the sleep that follows
when our bodies
touch

that moment
just before waking
when we realize
we've been holding one another
in our sleep

•

How do you use the word *love*
in a poem?

Love.

If you look at it
long enough
it will burn into your eyes

In the morning
when the house is quiet
I sit at the table

contemplate
                the old stove
how it glows
in first light

nothing is more white
more sure of itself
even the sunlight

bends around it
here
against the kitchen wall

COMMITMENT

I have decided
to live

    (with you)

you have agreed to take
out the trash (you don't
trust me with the garbagemen)
and I will put the toast
in the oven for breakfast
and coddle you
                  an egg
before you go to bed

we are wary   of being
            too close
            too often

we circle one another
like strange wolves
or people
       who know too much

I insist on separate rooms
you want your own typewriter
and ink your name on a cup
we hang our photographs   one
on top of the other and draw
lines on the whiskey bottle

but we will live together
and that is enough
when the sky unloads its snow
and the eyes move closer
to the fire

MARRIAGE: GETTING USED TO

It did not take me long
to get used to his leather
wings, no, they felt good
like an old, much-loved coat
draped over my shoulders
It was his feet I couldn't stand,
his horny feet, ugly as a bird's,
the yellow claws and the pride
he took in them:
> how he oiled the scales
> and saved the clippings,
> making me a necklace
> from the broken claws,
> sewing flakes of skin
> like sequins in my clothes

Even his tricks were okay
the way his words turned
to flames at parties,
sizzling flies from the air,
lighting cigarettes for ladies
with his tongue. It wasn't that
that bothered me

It was waking to find him
with a flashlight and a mirror,
staring under the covers at his feet
It was his nails
clicking across linoleum
It was the fallen gold scales
that lay on the sheet like scattered coins

in bed, does tricks, can
come on his head or
swinging from the light
enter me, a cork, Pop!
fills me up
or best when still
I move over him
my slippery skin, snake
swallows mouse, he dies
inside me often, I breathe
him into life, lick him
from darkness, his and mine
or just the night

YOU'RE SO COVERED WITH SCARS

You're so covered with scars
you forget where they come from.
Like birds they sing to the wounded
who descend from the railings of bridges
to follow you. In bars the cripples limp
to your table, drag their bleeding casts
towards the criss-cross of your face.
The old sit beside you in stations,
cough their lives into your lap. And now
I have come with my darkness to lie
against you. I trace the braille of your body:
the broken lip, the hole in the side
of your face. But you are emptied of stories.
Instead you press into my skin. The scars
cover me like feathers.

I WANT YOU

I want you
        to swallow me
        to carry me
inside   deeper than the last memory
of a mother whose earth-cracked
fingers clutched your hand
at the time of her dying

carry me
no matter where
my body takes me
or whom I love
for a moment
no matter what freedom
I seek from words
from syllables of stone

carry me
as the grass
        the deer's sleep
as the snow
        the wind's ribs

STILL-LIFE

When you are drunk with rage and fear
lower the glass bell over time

think of the stilled, the frozen
moment: the final second before

the bird's flight from the breathless
lake, the bee caught in the clear jar

the cat's body that melts
to bone under the steady sun

Those quiet moments when you don't know
I am looking: your hand poised above

the page before the first word or the last
the pause of the match held to your cigarette

as you lie naked after loving. When you are
mad with guilt and throw it like knives

pinning the hour-glass curve to the wall
hold these still-lifes in your hands

intervals of silence before you come
and the held breath breaks

We call this fear *love,* this tearing,
this fist, this sharpened tongue
love. I could kill you, I say,
many times. You do not carry
the only pain. There is more
than your world: the drunks
you find bleeding on the tiles,
the women full of holes, the dog
with torn eyes, the poet who has
chewed his tongue.

There is this room,
this woman who brings you food
wears your bruises on her cheeks.
I am tired, so tired.
There is always something wrong.
You spit words at me
like broken teeth and I, stupid
woman, string them into poems,
call them love.

I AM A LAKE

I am a lake
patterned by your tracks
across the snow sifted

to cross me
you must flop on your belly
like a seal   drag your massive weight
up my legs   across my chest
leaving a warm wide print
of your passage

if you insist
on walking
cracking jagged wounds
on my cold skin
with each thud of your heavy boots
I will open up   swallow you
hold you in my frozen mud
till spring

my fishes will lay eggs
in the cups of your eyelids
my lakebirds will nest in the hair
of your arms and your black thighs
the tongue of my water will ripple
your chest

after the thaw
as your feet send roots
through the softening mud
your fist will float to the surface
a tight white blossom
opening to the sun

beside the steel waters
three Eskimo girls
wait   silent
for the brown hands
to offer the fish eyes
that bind fisherman:girl
until the next catch

down your tongue
I roll the, eye
of the silver thrashing love
I hooked and gutted

scales dampen my palm

With your steps you measure
the ground our house will fill
knowing both of us have done this
with other people, in other places.
But this is different, we aren't young,
love isn't easy anymore.

By the cornerpost I find a grouse.
I touch the feathered eyelids,
think of the soft sleep the bird
has fallen into. In another place
I'd call it death but here
it is silence, a sense of peace.

Is this why we've come,
for something so simple?
A broken windmill, a dugout,
cold water from a well.

The house we have imagined
builds itself around us.
Like the bodies of lovers
who have been together years
the boards find their places,
fit snugly one against the other.
Stories rise above the trees;
doors and windows that have opened
inside us, open in the rooms
so all our empty spaces
fill with wind and light.

DEER MOUSE

Near the compost heap
a mouse builds a nest,
one door pointing north,
the other south.

A brown mouse
with white feet and russet ears
eyes that look at you
the way a deer does
when she thinks herself
invisible
in aspen shadows.

STUDY IN GREY

The great horned owl unrolls
her last long vowel to the tallow moon.
She abandons shadows, the light
and half-light of poplars around the empty house,
the broken plows and crockery,
the windmill that does not turn the wind.
No longer will she watch you search
through dust for pieces of your past.
She has seen her shadow nailed to the barn
and her young die in eggs that have no shells.

IN WHITE

The snowy owl flies
to the place where snow begins.
Only those pale as winter have survived:
the albino wolf, the sleek and silver fox.
But even where snow turns
everything to silence
and stills time like mercury
frozen in glass, she is not safe.
Across the moving ice
the white hunter drives his huskies
into her amber eyes.

SOUTH DAKOTA REFUGE

Go to Sand Lake, she says,
in November it's a platter
full of geese, your geese,
the Canadas come down with the snow,
feed on marsh grass
before their southern flight.

Along the border of the refuge:
wind off the lake, grey fog settling
on the water, the stir of wings.
Men warm their hands on thermoses,
cigarettes burn the morning air.
Against the cars like young boys,
bored, waiting for the end of silence,
the guns lean.

THE WEATHER

I want to wade in liquid heat,
submerge in the light
where all things are possible:
black birds turn iridescent,
finches flicker like candles
from green to green.
I want to believe in you.
I want your hands
to carry the sun to our bed.

Instead the cold follows us
like an old wrong we can't undo.
Christ, it's summer, we say,
thinking the word
will make it happen.

Even our faith in seasons
is misplaced. A hand moves across
a pencil drawing of the world
and smudges everything.

Let's catch minnows in a jar,
abandon our shoes on the bank
like an old sorrow, a heaviness.
Let's cross the creek
only for the sake of crossing
the slippery stones
which may or may not
hold our weight.

Though there's no time
to hesitate (all is in the movement,
the lack of pause) everything
at this moment
depends
on the firm and precise
placing of the
foot.

NO MATTER

No matter what happens
I will remember today
and remember it well.

The grey-striped cat
that moves so easy in her skin
caught a swallow
just learning to fly.

With stones we drove away
the gangly dog
no one would take home.
He watches from the woodpile,
ducks his head
when we talk too loud
or slam a door.

You sit alone in our cabin,
writing letters to another woman,
the address printed neatly
on a scrap of paper
I found and returned
to your pocket.

The dog would come
when we called
and eat our food
outside the kitchen door
after two weeks of pretending

we cared for its soft face,
its gibbled walk.

Every morning we watched
the swallow feed her young
in the mud nest below the dock.
And I was just beginning,
to learn to love
cats.

RAIN

So many write of rain
its small hands,
the memories it brings,
the sounds of things it touches.

How it changes what we see,
gives taste to what we thought
was tasteless: the grey of morning,
love's failures, the simple fear
of growing old
alone.

I think of this
as you drive away.
In the blacktop mirror
you are leaving
in the rain
you are leaving.

Your tail-lights burn
holes in the night
rain fills and spills from,
changing everything
except the songs
it carries to the earth.

ALICE

I know a woman
who can leave her body
and from the ceiling's corner
laugh at her mound of flesh
sweating on sheets

She looks like a normal woman
her eyes do not twist
nor does saliva thread
her chin   but sometimes when
we face in conversation
I feel her warm breath
on the back of my neck
and once I saw her laughing face
mirrored in her eyes

I have asked her
to teach me
to stride beyond this bone closet
but her act is instinctive
and beyond learning
or perhaps I am afraid
and don't really want to know
this final deception

For each time   she says
she stays away a little longer

THIS ONE'S FOR YOU

Hey, big hummer,
who can strut like you?
Crotch-tight jeans, boots
shiny as pool balls, heels
pounding stars into pavement
you call sky.

Hey, big rooster,
who can cockadoodledo
like you do? You raise the
bloody sun from his corner
your voice, brass
bell in the ring.

Hey, prize fighter,
who can screw like you?
Women howl your name,
say no man will take
your place, buzz them
like an electric drill.
You spin the world
on the end of your cock.

Hey, big talker,
waited all my life
for a man like you.
Come my way, I'll blow
the fuses in your big machine,
short all your circuits.
I'll break the balls
you rack on the table,
I'll bust your pool cue.

IN DARKNESS I WATCH YOU

Later, when you sleep with another,
tell her you have never loved
like this, I'll remember tonight
people sitting at your feet
listening to words
pulled through your fingers,
like touchstones
worried to the shape of your thoughts.

    This is fear, you say,
    and this. This is loneliness;
    the dark stone, despair.
    The one never found is love.

In darkness I watch you. I touch
the flower you bought in Old Montreal,
yellow petals turning brown, scent is
the last thing to die.

FLIGHT OF CRANES

A worm has eaten
the bud of the white peony
the Japanese call
                   Flight of Cranes.

What is left
is an empty shell
as if the heart of the flower
slithered out like a snail
forgetting to come home
after a night of wandering.

No cranes open their wings
on the peony tree
but perhaps the worm
fat on flowers
unfolds in threads of silk
as beautiful a name.

FISHING IN AIR

What he fishes for changes
as light changes on water.
Whitefish, pickerel, goldeye.
There is a space in his mind
where they die, a pier slippery with scales
where their eyes turn to slime.

His line is invisible.
He has forgotten what lure falls
endlessly through water.
It could be feathered or striped
or a silver curve that flashes
at the slightest flick of his wrist.

If he could send his eye out on a hook,
return it to its socket when he reels in the line,
he would do so. If he could use his heart for bait
then cut it from the fish within a fish.

There is something he has never caught.
Something that makes him stand here
every evening, casting, casting
and reeling in.

Every time he fishes he is different.
The water is different, the sky, the way
the tern hangs in the air or doesn't.
What he will catch is a minnow now,
slim and golden, growing to fill an emptiness
in a lake he's never seen before —
no road in or out.

DROUGHT

The hawk sits on the post,
head tucked in his shoulder.
It is mid-day. He knows the sun,
if he took flight, would singe
his wings and burn the moisture
from his eyes. Around him mice
crackle through the yellow grass,
their bodies small flames. Gophers
driven by the memory of seeds
move from darkness.

The hawk sleeps,
head tucked in his shoulder.
Soon he must hunt,
slice his wings through heat
that beats like rain
on the dry earth. His shadow
will offer the small
          a moment's respite
before he drops and drinks.

LOON SONG

The loon has left its voice
and flown away.
I hear it in the early light
and just before sleeping,
rolling through reeds towards the shore.

It lives in the lake
and sometimes in the mind.
Now it sits in the belly
of a rainbow trout
moving like memory through darkness.

If you can empty yourself,
lay your senses around you
like five white cups,
it will build a nest in one of them.

You will see the distances
only birds know, feel the loneliness
that rose from the long dark throat
before the loon, weary of its voice,
flew away.

III

The Morning of the Sad Women

THE MORNING OF THE SAD WOMEN

Morning holds its mirror
to the window, the women
wake to their own reflections,
fall into loneliness deeper
than the night they rose from.
They reach for housecoats,
brush the tangles from their hair
as if there were a chance
of meeting someone in the hall.

If it is winter, the rooms are dark.
Clocks count heartbeats
in the glow of bedside lamps.
Albums hold their secrets
in dresser drawers, press
the photographs so thin
there is little left of them.

Downstairs no one is making breakfast,
no one brings oranges on a silver tray.
Morning makes a poor companion
when there is nowhere to go with it,
when it repeats the same
conversations across the narrow table
over and over without end.

The wild geese fly
the same pathways
they have followed for centuries.

There is comfort in this
though they are not the same
geese my mother listened to
when she was young.

Perhaps I first heard them
inside her
as she watched their wings
eclipse the moon, their call
the first sound — separate
from the soft, aquatic
whispers of the womb.

And my sadness is her sadness
passed through generations
like distance and direction
and the longing
for the nesting ground.

MOTHER IS SEWING

Mother is sewing
a wedding dress.

The stitches are her sighs
as she rises in the dark
to start the fire
and call the children
from their sleep.

Against my skin the cloth
is blue and cool as the water
I raise to wash my breasts
at night
when the others are in bed.

In each seam she sews a seed,
two from the poplar
outside my window,
leaves eaten by worms
the last three summers

a juniper berry
saved from the one time
father drove her
to the Cypress Hills

the seeds of fireweed
from ditches along our road.

She tells me
they'll start growing

on my wedding night
fill my house
with leaves and flowers,
blue-green berries
that cover barren places.

Mother is sewing
my wedding dress.

The thread is time.
Where she knots it,
it makes an end.

STILLBORN

who
looped the cord
around his fine new neck

who
hanged him
in my bone gallows   my

beautiful son
blue as the blue
in Chinese porcelain

To find words
large enough to hold
the dead. Twenty-two young men
from the steel gang of the CPR
killed on highway number one.

My words cannot contain their lives.
I do not know their names,
the stories they liked to tell
after a hard day on the line,
the way they held their cigarettes,
the family pictures in their wallets.
I do not know them

can think of nothing
but the charred bodies
pulled from the wreck
and laid between blue lines
in the hockey rink

the only place in town
large and cold enough
to hold them.

THE CHILD WHO WALKS BACKWARDS

My next-door neighbour tells me
her child runs into things.
Cupboard corners and doorknobs
have pounded their shapes
into his face. She says
he is bothered by dreams,
rises in sleep from his bed
to steal through the halls
and plummet like a wounded bird
down the flight of stairs.

This child who climbed my maple
with the sureness of a cat,
trips in his room, cracks
his skull on the bedpost,
smacks his cheeks on the floor.
When I ask about the burns
on the back of his knee,
his mother tells me
he walks backwards
into fireplace grates
or sits and stares at flames
while sparks burn stars in his skin.

Other children write their names
on the casts that hold
his small bones.
His mother tells me
he runs into things,
walks backwards,
breaks his leg
while she lies
sleeping.

DEEP WELL

When I die
do not bury me
Stretch my arms above my head
Let my hands sound one silent clap
Bind them with a leather thong
Sharpen them to ten hard points
When I have stiffened
drag my body to the highest hill
Start the machinery
Let my body twist and turn
a flesh drill
spinning through the topsoil the sand
the heavy black clay
Let my fingers touch the way down
through fossils
through the final soggy layers
to the underground lake
Let me splash through cold dead waters
Let me be a blind fish
belly up
bumping my nose on other creatures of the dark

THE WOMEN WHO SURVIVE

My mother and my aunt
talk of disaster
they are that old now
they talk of death
every morning over coffee
the same dark chant

Scotty MacKay, you know him, he's the third uncle of your
cousin twice removed, perfectly healthy man, went down the
basement to change the filter in the furnace, when he didn't
come up for supper, his wife went down and found him dead.
Remember Alf Tone, my aunt says, I'm sure he was murdered,
they found him in the cistern where he'd been for two months.
Not murdered, says my mother, he was probably just cleaning
it and his heart gave out.
No, he had his going-to-town clothes on, no one cleans the
cistern with their going-to-town clothes on.

It's always the men
who die, they keel over
at the breakfast table
breaking poached eggs
with their foreheads
or they fall in the shower
clutching ropes of water

So unexpected, say
my mother and my aunt
nibbling date squares
left over from the funerals
Why, I saw him only yesterday
It just goes to show you

1

Cleat McLeod saw
the storm coming
He wrapped his arms
around the stall post
and yelled to his wife
running for the root cellar
          If the barn goes
          I go with it

He and the post
were ten feet off the ground
before he could let go

2

The south edge of the cyclone
lifted Teman Leep's
new hip-roofed barn
Wind and land
clapped their hands together
smashed the building flat

The old tumble-down house
his wife wished would fall
stood firm

3

The wind lifted
Prine Gossard's house
so all the furniture
                    slid to one side

Granny Gossard
rode her rocking chair
right through the parlour window
She only broke a leg

4

Shorty Turnbull refused
to stop plowing
His hired hand ran
to the rock pile
          (later over a beer
          in Stanley Buck's basement
          he said *First time I've*
          ever been thankful
          for a rock)
and hung on

The wind lifted
horse, man and plow
set them in Sylvester's field
seven miles away

Turnbull plowed his neighbour's
quarter section
before he knew
where he was

5

On the way down the cellar
Esther Simmie's new
store-bought hat
blew back East
where it came from

Next year, a storm
blew in from the opposite direction
Her husband caught the hat
as it sailed by the house

6

Everyone lived to tell
even the old Dutchman's wife
who was struck by lightning
(the only woman for miles
so lonely
she followed his plow like a dog)

She wasn't killed
but she's walked stooped ever since

7

Hens were lifted up
like cottonwood fluff
and gently lowered
to the east of the yard

After that taste of flying
those hens never laid good again

but kept on flapping
blunt wings
like headless chickens
trying to rise above
their own blood

8

Like an animal compelled
to return and tear apart
the cage that held it
the wind
doubled the windmill tower
like a wishbone
and planted its blades
in the dark mud

9

The Model T
never moved

THE FAT LADY'S DANCE

The fat lady can't get out of bed.
He has done it before, his idea of a joke.
He has left her there and gone to work
after he has watched each greasy egg
slither down her throat, after he has made her
swallow every wad of buttered bread.

When she hears the door close, she snivels,
she starts to cry as she always does.
But something strange begins to happen.
Somewhere under the globs of flesh
she feels a motion, a memory of movement.
The fat lady thinks of feet.
She stops crying,
opens her mouth, sucks in all
the rage her belly can hold.
With a massive heave-ho she rolls
off the bed to the floor and goes on rolling
splits the door frame with her legs
crumbles the wall with her shoulders
crashes through the living room
onto the steps and rolls down the street.

Cars skid out of her way,
she caroms off a bus
and on she rolls, her flesh
slaps the pavement,
children follow her booming parade,
dogs bark at her one-piece band.
She fells trees, she bursts hydrants
she rolls through the town
and up to the door of his office.

With one great yell, one mighty heave
she rolls the building flat
then rises up on jiggling legs
and shaking the brick dust off her nightgown
she pirouettes out of town.

mother was a lovely beast
she gave to me a lovely feast
three teats hanging from her chest
I found the third one quite the best

a coarse black beard grew from her chin
she worried it was due to sin
but she was good and she was kind
and father didn't seem to mind

with three tits you can suckle three
and still leave room enough for me
besides, you're quiet as a flower
a wife's tongue makes marriage sour

he stroked her beard as she stroked his
they lived a life of total bliss
till people came from field and town
to see my mother's chest and down

so father built a stage for her
to bare her breasts and show her fur
he tried to teach her how to scowl
to walk on fours, to moan and growl

she sat on stage head-bowed, alone
while father bought a megaphone
The Bearded Venus he would say
A Woman — and he'd make them pay

still mother uttered not a sound
but when my father went uptown

she raised her skirts to show her hair
and let men mount her like a mare

mother was a lovely beast
she gave to me a lovely feast
three teats hanging from her chest
I found the third one quite the best

BURNING

she hides inside
her burns
yellowing blistered draining
her eyes escaped the fire
she sees you
sitting beside her bed

they have told you
her brain is
alive   somewhere
behind the eyes

you want to cut a hole
in the top of her head
drag her out
but you are afraid   to touch
her skin may stick
to your fingers

they have told you
a burn is a slow
dying
it only kills
one person   at a time

one of her is
already dead

FORTRESS

She builds a house,
a solid house of fieldstones
heaved by muscles of ice
from the dark earth below
The clay from her garden
is mortar packed black
between the rocks
Around the house she piles
a wall   white buffalo bones
dragged from bushed hollows
near rocks rubbed smooth
by matted backs,
a wall six feet high
skull on skull thigh locked into thigh
sky in eye sockets and open jaws

She builds no gate
but in the one round window
she hangs a candle
on a leather rope
She embroiders sunflowers
on white shirts
and over the open fire
she dries her hair
to thatch the roof

For these women the garden is everything.
The flowers a country of sorrow, of longing,
a language sweet and foreign on the tongue.
Beside pools where carp grow fat on bread,
they arrange the perfumed blossoms of their skin
in light the leaves turn over
like fingers testing the richness of silk.
Here paths turn back on themselves
under the perfect circles the trees
are twisted into. The women pretend beauty,
imagine passion, fall into the gentle
sadness of the flesh. Figs and sweetmeats,
blood oranges, black olives, wine.
Above garden walls the moon rises
impersonal as desire. The women seduce
their own reflections, leaves curl inward,
petals close like mouths.

Pale arms, weary at their sides, still
as grass snakes in the thin grass shadows,
they hear only the faintest sound of music
as their ears fill with dirt. Waiting
for their strong thighs to sink into earth,
waiting for lichens to weave delicate
circles on the stones of their ankles,
they all lie still.

Until wind takes what is left,
plucks the bright dresses from the bones,
whirls them, twirls them
topples them up
and down
         over the dirt fields
to the windows of the farm houses
where wives who scald sealers
and knead dough with strong hands
raise their heads
move their feet to the window
cry
    Look, the wind
    is a woman
    and she dances.

IV

The Garden Going On Without Us

From *The Sex Lives of Vegetables*

CARROTS

Carrots are fucking
the earth. A permanent
erection, they push deeper
into the damp and dark.
All summer long
they try so hard to please.
Was it good for you,
was it good?

Perhaps because the earth won't answer
they keep on trying.
While you stroll through the garden
thinking *carrot cake,*
carrots and onions in beef stew,
carrot pudding with caramel sauce,
they are fucking their brains out
in the hottest part of the afternoon.

Radishes flip their skirts in the wind
like a line of chorus girls
throw them over their heads.

If they were singers
they'd be the Andrews sisters.
If they had jobs
they'd be nurses who drive
red sports cars after work.

Every spring you put up with
their flirtations
for the crunch between your teeth
the quick surprise
                    of rain and fire
they've saved all season
just for you.

CABBAGES

Long-living and slow,
content to dream in the sun,
heads tucked in, cabbages
ignore the caress of the
cabbage butterfly, the soft
sliding belly of the worm.

You know it's crazy
but they lie so still,
so self-contained, you imagine them
laying eggs
in the earth's dark pockets,
expect one morning they'll be gone,
dragging themselves
to the creek behind the house,

making their way
with great deliberation
to the sea.

LETTUCE

Raised for one thing
and one thing only,
lettuce is a courtesan
in her salad days.
Under her fancy crinolines
her narrow feet are bound.

CAULIFLOWER

The garden's pale brain,
it knows the secret
lives of all the vegetables,
holds their fantasies,
their green libidos
in its fleshy lobes.

The onion loves the onion.
It hugs its many layers,
saying O, O, O,
each vowel smaller
than the last.

Some say it has no heart.
It doesn't need one.
It surrounds itself,
feels whole. Primordial.
First among vegetables.

If Eve had bitten it
instead of the apple,
how different
Paradise.

TOMATOES

Pixie. Pretty Patio.
Red Cushion. No wonder
they all have round heels
and rouge their nipples.

YAMS

Sweet potatoes, yams,
what delights they hide
inside their dappled jackets

hot from the oven
steaming in the bowl
at the first
              touch
of the knife
              they flash
orange flesh

what pleasures

they expose
to our tongues

POTATOES

No one knows
what potatoes do.
Quiet and secretive
they stick together.
So many under one roof
there is talk of incest.

The pale, dumb faces,
the blank expressions.
Potato dumplings.
Potato pancakes.
Potato head.

In dark cellars
they reach across the potato bin
to hold one another
in their thin white arms.

CUCUMBERS

Cucumbers hide
        in a leafy camouflage,
popping out
when you least expect
like flashers in the park.

The truth is,
they all have an anal
fixation. Watch it
when you bend to pick them.

BRUSSELS SPROUTS

Brussels sprouts are Siamese
twins joined at the spine.
If you ask one out
you have to take the lot.
Do you have a sister?
sends them into giggling fits.

They all wear matching
sweater sets and sunglasses,
the reflecting kind,
so they see themselves
                                   looking back
from the flat surface
of each other's eyes.

ARTICHOKES

Artichokes never
take off their clothes.
They want seduction,
melted butter, a touch
of wild garlic.

PEAS

Peas never liked any of it.
They make you suffer for the sweet
burst of green in the mouth. Remember
the hours of shelling on the front steps,
the ping into the basin? Your mother
bribing you with lemonade to keep you there,
splitting them open with your thumbs.

Your tongue finds them clitoral
as it slides up the pod.
Peas are not amused.
They have spent all their lives
keeping their knees together.

ZUCCHINI

The zucchini strokes the slim waists
of the pea vines, peeks under
the skirts of the yellow beans,
squares its shoulders and says to the rhubarb,
There's only room for one of us.

But mainly it is passive,
a voyeur lying still and silent
in its speckled lizard skin.

In secret shadows it spreads
like must over the garden,
the zucchini's eyes are open all night.

PUMPKINS

Pumpkins are the garden's
huge guffaw.
                    Toothy grins
splitting their cheeks
long before
you carve a face.

They roll on the ground
holding their sides,
deep belly laughter
rising in waves slapping
drum-barrel chests
like water in a bucket.

They are laughing
                    the last laugh
the ludicrous genital
tug and pull of things

laughing with the moon-mad
melons
            spilling like breasts
from the earth's popped buttons.

WATERMELONS

The watermelon is full
of mouths and small black teeth
sucked smooth
as pebbles from a stream.

It is waiting for you
to rap on its door,
waiting to give you
a juicy hello
                    smack!
right on the lips

a kiss so sweet
you'll keep coming back
for more.

SCARLET RUNNER BEANS

Lyricists and scribes
scarlet runner beans
illuminate the vegetable
book of hours

transcribe
with slender fingers
what tomato says
to sweet basil,
cardamom to carrot,
dill to courting bee.

In perfect longhand
they write couplets
make puns on *pistil*

articulate
              erotic chlorophylls
almost visible
on the wind's turning pages.

DELIGHT IN THE SMALL, THE SILENT

Delight in the small,
those that inhabit
only a corner of the mind,
the ones shaped by wind
and a season: a slip of
grass, the nameless flower
that offers its scent
to a small wind

Delight in the silent,
the ones that change shape
soundlessly as moons:
the fossil golden bee
caught in amber, the bone
transmuted to stone, the
chrysalis of the gypsy moth

Delight in flesh
that does not turn to
word, the ones without
voice or master. The old dog
who denies name, moves
arthritic legs to whatever
you choose to call him

Weary of men, of words
carved even in the penis
bones of bears, delight
in the small, the silent
whose language lies

in their doing and their
undoing, those who turn
to stone to bone to wing
without a shout of praise
find their perfect form
become imago

GLOVES

The gardeners, old-country and tired,
plant their worn and loamy leather gloves,
the tannin good for growing
like soot, grass clippings, the ground
hooves of horses. Imagine all those
gloves stripped of flesh and bone
buried deep in the earth. Hollow fingers
slightly bent, an abacus of leather
knuckles, cracked palms — lifelines gone mad.
One glove holds the roots of a rose
like a tangle of veins. In another
a striped beetle builds a world from everything
the hand has touched. A star-nosed mole,
blind and dreamy, makes of one
a hammock for its noon-day naps.
Other gloves pass memories like prize squash
from hand to hand: the year of the bad frost,
the wind storm that pulled up the radishes,
the tomato blight. These are the ones
that want to go back to the hoe and trowel,
the sweat white on their palms
when the work was done,
the shed where they hung for years
from a nail like caught bats.

GARDEN IN WINTER

The woman blind from birth
turns the pages of a seed catalogue
mailed from a place
far south of here.

Her fingers dream a garden
out of winter, stroke
the red and orange of poppies,
the blue of phlox, the other
blue of gentians
                but in her garden
everything is white
as though an early storm
shrouded all the plants with snow,
shapes soft and indistinct
and shifting in the wind.

To walk through her garden
is to fall into a pillow,
to look down the throat of a calla lily.
The shadows are white,
that is to say, there are no shadows
just light
like nothing ever seen before.

Imagined light
                pure and crystal
emptied of everything
but itself.

GARDEN AT NIGHT

Leaves flood the yard
in deep shadows. Gourds
float like jellyfish
in the night's tidal pools.

This far from the ocean
only plants know
such darkness.

Even the earthworm
pulls threads of light
through the blackest corner,
the sleeping eye.

ANIMALS OF SPRING

You want to take them in
let them sleep in your bed,
purr on your kitchen counter.
You dip your hand in honey.
Tongues lick your fingers,
tickle your palm. You feed them
cubes of sugar, milk from an eye dropper,
you tie ribbons in their hair.

These are the half-formed,
the helpless, some are blind.
But soon they take their shape,
eyes open, listen to the voice
that stirs inside them. It says
wind, snow. It says meat, mate,
hunt, marrow.

They grow to fill your house
as goldfish fill the space they live in.
But these are not goldfish
trapped in a bowl. These are
the animals of spring, the ones you found
playing in the forest, the teddy-bears
you take to bed, the kittens you tease
with skeins of wool.

                One day
when you honey your fingers,
offer the sweetness to be licked,
your hand will disappear.

The animals of summer lie in the coulee's dip,
the cool shadow. Delicately with their teeth,
lips curled back, they pluck berries from branches.
You watch them from the hill. You are not afraid.
Their teeth pick berries, chew ripe flesh, the stone.
They rise, stretch their legs straight in front,
open mouths, yawn. The animals of the lengthening day
move slowly, they survived the winter, the young
wrestle at the mouth of the cave.

They could be house-cats, they could be dogs.
But you watch them from the hill,
know you are there because the wind
blows your smell behind you. Know you are there
because it's summer and it's morning. In moonlight
the animals change their shape, remember blood,
remember bone, sniff the ground where you sat.
Lips pulled back, their teeth burn like stars.

IN MOONLIGHT

Something moves
just beyond the mind's
clumsy fingers.

It has to do with seeds.
The earth's insomnia.
The garden going on
without us

needing no one
to watch it

not even the moon.

Even the dead reach for you
as you walk, so beautiful,
across the earth.

Their fingers turn to flowers
as they break through
the soil, touch the air.

The bouquets in your room
are the hands of the dead,
transmuted. Roses.

Salal. Gladioli.
Scent covers you, a fine dust.
Leaves move in benediction.

Even the dead bless you.
Their blossoms glow
like muted lanterns

lighting your way
as you walk
green paths of sleep.

RETURNING

"Could we go back
To the old garden, we should not stay long;
The fruit that we should find would all be fallen,
And have the taste of earth." — E. A. Robinson

I

It is difficult to write
of this return:

Dust settles in my throat
Ditches are burnt black
Grass and weeds
grow too high   will trap
the snow and block
the only road from town

2

To drop into the past effortlessly
To walk through the yard past rusted
machinery, gutted stoves, broken windows
To fall through rotted boards into the dry well
landing at the bottom
soft as down

3

The way back: the tracks
fill with snow   a whiteness
swallows the road
what is ahead or behind

The right tires sink
in the hidden ditch
I imagine my body's
freezing   the skin
thick as grapefruit rinds

I push and shovel
until fingers numb
I sit in the car
Darkness surrounds me
with wings   shadows in snow

I turn on the radio
know he will come
pull me out with his heavy chain
pull me home

4

We see breath clouds
before the deer, sense warmth
before movement

I will be breath
melting the ice behind his eyes
warming his throat
with my speaking

5

He has planted
rows and rows of trees
siberian elm   black poplar   caragana
chokecherry   spruce
He has changed
the shape of my sky

6

When you were away
he says
          the wind rose

Windows moved in and out
Shingles were crows in the wind
The caraganas were stripped
like sun-peeled skin
The spruce upended and our land
blew five miles down the road

That is why I moved the house

Now do you understand?

7

Not even this body
is familiar

Thinner
          (eat better since

you left. Two vegetables
per meal, no crumb cakes,
New York Delight, or apple
crisp pudding)
he runs every morning
uphill   against the wind
the sun a steam-roller
on his back

I can roll my fist
in the hollow of his chest
cup his hip bones in my hands
Our ribs lock together

Not even this body
                    is safe

8

I will be the butterfly
my pattern unrepeated
Just one wing

I will light
on the lined skin
below his eye
                delicate
as lost words we both
remember

I will be beautiful
because I won't be whole
Unsuitable
for glass or frame

9

The first morning
I vacuum corners, watch addresses
shrivel in fire, shine
each splattered mirror
He knows me
by smell, the kitchen sounds,
the bend of my body in sleep

And now I sleep more
except at night when I stand
at the southern window,
listen to the panic of wings

10

The dog will not come

sits in the corner, snarls
when I pass
Today as I lower her dish
she tries to bite me
clamps her teeth on my sleeve
hangs like a funeral bell

She remembers my leaving

11

I will be
the tongue of a bird
curled in the cage
of his hands
                singing

12

I fold his T-shirts
place them on his shelves
The cotton is warm from the dryer
stained from his mixing of colours
The smell is clean
as billowed snow

Today I unpack
the last suitcase
carry it hollow
down the basement

13

He warms the car
scrapes frost in the dark mornings
doesn't speak
                    before breakfast

I toast the bread
crack eggs into the oiled pan

Our snares of words
no longer tighten or choke
the air between us

Like wild creatures, we know
when to circle   approach
downwind slow

We live in the comfort
where night touches
mute
as wings of moths

V

What the Mind Turns Over

What the mind turns over
and over like polished stones
are the blue butterflies
rising from grass
as we passed the altars.

At Uxmal we listened
to the old stories:
the butterflies are souls
of those the priests
tore open, hearts beating
high in the sun. The ruins
are memories now, here
where snow drifts by the windows.

Across the room shadows
touch your face.
Wings open and close
like fragile hands,
delicate as frost
forming on glass.

As you fall asleep,
they brush my skin,
settle in my hair.
Nothing that moves
is so blue.

PAVLOVA

Even you, Pavlova, you
with the beautiful feet and arms,
even you did not die
with grace or beauty.
Your last words
Get my swan costume ready
were what we would have written
for you, but death would not
lift you weightless
into the bright air.

You waited
in the shadows of the wings,
moistening your lips,
crossing yourself as you had
a hundred times before.
Should I have had children instead?
Sons and daughters
to show pictures to.
This is the country I left,
see why I weep.

In Russia the snow is falling
as it does in memory, falling
on the backs of horses,
settling in the furs of women
who ride to the concert halls.
In your garden in England
the swan who laid his neck
across your shoulders

134

and bit your flesh
in his dark unpredictable beak
dreams himself whole again
up to where the sky
was made for swans.

Lonely and sick you lie
in a Dutch hotel.
Your lungs like stones
press you into the bed.
Clutching your husband's hand,
you feel the warmth of the mistress
he left just moments ago,
hear his words
She will not dance tomorrow,
as the doctor cuts
into your ribcage
to drain the pus
and let the breath in.

Three sounds beneath the mountain:
a stream over stones,
the clacking of looms,
the younger woman laughing.

She is sixty-five
and still an apprentice.
It may be years before
she takes the name of her teacher.
Or it may be tomorrow.
Her teacher is ninety.
Her hands know everything,
they move with the quickness
of wrens.

Outside the hut, the wind
has found a form to take.
It sways on the line,
long strips of bright
cotton. The evening settles
like a dove over the valley,
the looms are silent. One woman
stirs dye in a wooden vat.
The other carries cloth
to the mountain stream.

Every day the old one grows
in the other's eyes.
There is much to learn
and much to teach

here
where all things are:

the mountain,
the stream flowing from it,
two women at the centre,
all the blue of the world
flowing through their veins
into cloth
for those who live in cities
they have no need to see.

His handwriting jumps with his heart,
chamois leaping the stretch of paper,
the mind's snowy plain. He is weeping.
His wife won't learn how to dance.
Red roses frighten him, his love is white.
He has drawn Christ without a beard,
without a moustache. Who dares to look
at the naked face? Nijinsky, his round eyes.
Man is not a monkey, man is God,
God is not a monkey. To make the mind
white, to dance on pins, to dance
on a madman's nerves. *I look like Him*
only He has a calm gaze and my eyes are round.
His mind jumps with his writing. In his diary
a red rose burns, it eats the air.
Around it ashes and wounds. His fingers ache
when they touch his forehead. It is naked.
Where is the white between words,
between breath and breath? His heart
jumps in his chest, it lifts him high
above the trees, his feet on fire,
they are turning into roses and burning.
Below him the town with its little houses,
all the windows lit. Inside one he imagines
his wife turning the pages of a diary. His love
is white and far away. He moves his feet to music.
Between everything from this distance
there is only snow.

The first time his grandfather beat him,
he lay in bed for five days, listened
to Grandmother telling stories
and speaking her own words to God.

His heart grew eyes and ears.
It put on shoes and walked through every room,
heard Aunt Natalya's crying, the laughter
as his uncles teased blind Grigori,
heating the handles of his scissors,
placing the slop pail in his path.
Grigori told him, *Look them straight in the eye.
Even a mad dog will turn away.*

The hours of sickness dragged through him,
sledges pulled through heavy snow.
As the walls of his heart grew thinner,
things became clear: Aunt Natalya's death
in childbirth, his mother's leaving,
but he never understood why his grandmother,
so strong and wise, allowed her husband
to beat her.

It was she who told the neighbours
what to do for disputes, for lice:
*Wash often at the bathhouse, my dear,
and best to steam yourself with oil of peppermint.*
One shout from Grandmother and the devil
who scraped his tail across the roof
somersaulted to earth and disappeared.
She had seen angels and talked to saints

as if they were cousins stopping in for a visit
on their way to the city.

But Grandfather knew all the letters.
E for ever; F for father.
Learn them, Aloysha, then we'll learn the prayers.

While Grandmother listened, hands clasped
in her lap as if she held something precious,
Aloysha looked the old man in the eye,
shouted the letters from his bed
until they scraped his throat like raw potatoes,
shouted to his grandfather
who beat them and knew the right way
to talk to God.

THE MAGICIAN

When the magician left, he forgot
to join the sawed woman. The upper-half
asleep in her box, did not see him go.
But when she awoke, she knew —
all the rabbits had disappeared,
his cape had been pulled from the laundry basket
and the house was clear of smoke. For days
her head screamed, her legs kicked the box
but no one came.

When the magician remembered,
he cancelled his travelling band and returned home.
The lower box was empty, but the eyes
in the head opened and the woman said,
It's too late now. I've found a rat
for a lover. He's eaten my most delicate bits.
When he has swallowed my tongue,
we'll sing you a song of bone. The wind,
my rat lover and me.

The magician buried her head in the yard,
covered her grave with stones,
but stones couldn't hold down the wind
or still the rat
building its tangled nest behind her eyes.

THE FLOWERS OF GEORGIA O'KEEFFE

The nasturtium with its round leaves
sucks the bee inside, becomes an O'Keeffe
blossom hung on the wall of the sky.
Light spills from each petal, gathers
at the soft, sweet centre. There sits
Sigmund Freud where he's always wanted
to be, whispering secret words as the bee
fills its sack with pollen.

Georgia O'Keeffe walks her dog
through the mesas where everything blooms.
Somewhere a painting begins.
It makes its first strokes across the canvas,
flowers open their mouths, bees mount stamens.
Freud checks his pocket watch, wonders
what his wife will make for dinner,
whispers *shit, cunt, fuck,* the bee
drowning in pollen. In the desert
Georgia watches the dome of a skull
rising like a moon over the horizon.
Her dog sleeps among succulents. Roses
lift his eyes to heaven.

Freud dreams himself inside a flower,
red and redolent with light.
Somewhere his wife is singing
but he doesn't hear. Too many
flowers in his garden. Too many bees
drunk on pollen. The blooms are hysterical.
They make his head hurt.

A Note on the Text

"The Morning of the Sad Women" was inspired by David Wagoner's "The Evening of the Sad Women."

Some of the poems in this book have been selected from the following books: *Crow's Black Joy* (NeWest Press, 1978); *Humans and Other Beasts* (Turnstone Press, 1980); *No Longer Two People,* with Patrick Lane (Turnstone Press, 1981); *The Weather* (Coteau Books, 1984).

Other poems collected here for the first time have appeared or are about to appear in: *Poetry Canada Review; Canadian Poetry Now; Cross Canada Writers' Quarterly; Arts Manitoba; Room of One's Own; Malahat Review; The Canadian Forum; Prairie Fire; NeWest Review; Event; Waves; Women and Words: The Anthology.*

Many thanks to Donna Bennett for her encouragement and expert editing; to the Poets' Combine for their advice, and to the Saskatchewan Writers'/Artists' Colonies. I am also grateful to the Saskatchewan Arts Board, the Canada Council, and the Regina Public Library for their financial support which made the writing of the book possible.

Lorna Crozier
July 1985